THRIVING IN
QUARANTINE

**A Humorous Look at One Family's
Misadventures Aboard the Corona Cruise**

I wish you joy in your journey

Barney Cargile

Barney Cargile

THRIVING IN QUARANTINE
BY BARNEY CARGILE

ISBN:
Copyright © 2020 by Barney Cargile
Cover design by Jennifer Burrell
Interior design by Joe Sade

For more information on this book and the author visit: Barney-Cargile.com

Dedication

This book is dedicated to the love of my life, the beautiful woman who has stood beside me for forty-six years, even during the Corona Cruise. She constantly inspires me, and is my muse in every aspect of my life. (In case you haven't figured it out, that would be my wife Linda.)

Contents

Prologue

On Friday, February 21, 2020, the *Gran Princess* set sail for the Hawaiian Islands, with approximately 2,400 passengers aboard. Among them were Barney and Linda Cargile, along with their daughter, Tiffany Essig, and her husband, Scott. Their children—Olive (eight years old), Liam (six years old), and Olin (one-year-old)—accompanied them. The cruise promised fifteen days of luxurious pampering and relaxation. After all, the Princess Cruise Lines motto declares, "Come Back New." Every passenger aboard the ship did exactly that, only not quite as they expected.

On March 23, our family was among the first passengers to return home, after six days of quarantine aboard the ship and fourteen days at Travis Air Force Base. This is the story of one family's adventure—an ordeal they have affectionately dubbed The Corona Cruise. This account does not represent everyone's experience; it primarily reflects the author's viewpoint. I refer to this book as "a humorous look," but no one in our family found humor in those who became ill or died from COVID-19. Rather, this book is a humorous look at our family's experience. All the events in this book actually occurred; however, the author freely acknowledges the use of artistic license in recounting them. Enjoy.

Chapter One

A FISH IN A BARREL

S eptember 17, 2019. The laundry-room door creaked open. Since no tiny footsteps followed, I concluded the visitor was not one of the grandkids. My son-in-law, Scott, was at work. The goats were in the field. So my Sherlock Holmes senses kicked in, and I deduced it must be my daughter, Tiffany. Engrossed in Mike Rowe's *The Way I Hear It*, I ignored the intrusion. Besides, I was just getting to the proverbial good part of the story.

Tiffany had open access to our home because my wife, Linda, and I lived next to Tiffany's family in adjoining units of a duplex. Linda and I had purchased the property, which sat on two-and-a-half acres, eight years earlier. Tiffany and Scott's family occupied one side of the duplex; Linda and I lived in the other half. In addition to incredibly low housing costs for the wine country of Sonoma County, the living arrangements were a sweet deal in other ways as well. Scott and Tiffany benefited from perpetually free babysitting, and Linda and I received … I'm not exactly sure what we received unless I count the gourmet meals Tiff cooked for us each night and the continual litany of tech perplexities I presented to Scott, as well as the blessing of watching our grandchildren grow up every day.

"Hi, Dad," Tiff said, in a singsong voice, rivaling Lady Gaga. "How's the best dad in the world doing?"

I jolted upright. She sounded entirely too happy for a cloudy day. If she was that euphoric, she should be home baking me a peach cobbler. Something sneaky was afoot.

"Hey, Sweetie. What do you need?"

"I don't need anything. Just wanted to bring this peach cobbler over for you."

My skeptical meter spiked. Linda then stepped into view. The two of them were up to something. "Okay. What do you want?" I asked suspiciously, sensing this was about to cost me money.

"Well, Dad. Now that you mention it, there is one teeny, tiny favor you might be able to do for us."

I instinctively reached for my wallet, like one of Pavlov's dogs drooling over meat.

Her words rushed out. "You know how it's my fortieth birthday in a few months—"

I almost blurted, "Yes, I was there," but wisely kept my mouth shut.

"—And that Scott and I just celebrated our tenth anniversary? Well, we are planning to go on a cruise and bring the kids with us."

For a moment, my world brightened. The word *staycation* raced through my brain like a shooting star. I envisioned days of lounging on our deck in my briefs, sipping iced tea. No back-washing from tiny mouths that sampled my libations—the owners of those mouths would all be sailing the high seas.

"Well, I called Princess Cruises to get a quote. They have some really great deals right now. You can get a fifteen-day cruise to Hawaii really cheap. And it costs almost nothing to add on the kids. They're so excited!"

Her obsessive attention to details worried me. And why in the name of Neptune would you inform kids ahead of time you were taking them on a cruise? That sort of information should only be revealed five minutes before you pull out of the driveway.

"Okay," I mumbled. My amygdala shot out a warning that I'd

better start paying close attention. I sensed a bank loan could be forthcoming.

"Well ..." she said.

Tiffany was beginning every sentence with *well*. A sure sign of nervous awkwardness.

"It turns out that we can only have two kids to a cabin, and since we have three kids—"

"You won't be going?" I interrupted.

"Well, only if you can't help us." Tiff twisted her features into that pouty-little-girl face no father can resist. "I know you and Mom have been saving up for a cruise next year." She paused and took a deep breath. Then exhaling, she shot out at light-speed, "Would you be willing to go with us and have one of the kids registered to your room? It would only be a technicality. Once we're onboard, all the kids would be in our room."

I shot Linda a glance. She merely nodded. Mother and daughter had already formed a traitorous treaty, and I had been ambushed by their deception.

"But we were planning to go to the Panama Canal," I protested. "Besides, we don't have the money." I raised my eyebrows at Linda in victory.

Then Linda stepped in for round two. "Barney, I don't really wanna go to the Panama Canal. It sounds boring." She and I had discussed the Panama Canal cruise for months, so her revelation sent me reeling.

"Does it really matter where we go?" Linda asked. "Won't it be great just to get away? The open seas. The romance of Hawaii at sunset. We'll hardly even see the kids. Besides, it's not for several months. We'll have the money by then. We can give it to each other for Christmas. You won't have to buy me a present. That'll save us a lot."

The odds of that happening were as likely as Sylvester Stallone starring in a chick flick. "Let me think about it." Maybe I could stall long enough for the excitement to blow over.

"Sure," Tiff said. "You and mom discuss it."

I knew only too well how that conversation would turn out.

As she walked away, Tiffany threw a deadly verbal hand grenade. "Just remember. The kids are *so* excited. You wouldn't want to keep them from their dream trip."

My options had evaporated. Like a fish in a barrel, I'd been hooked.

Chapter Two

GET READY TO CRUISE

As soon as the door closed behind Tiffany, Linda turned on her feminine charms. Kissing me, she said, "Whatever you decide is okay with me. I just wanna tell you, though, the grandkids are really excited. But I'll leave it up to you."

I winced. How could I possibly combat the grandkids card? "Linda, you realize we'll end up babysitting. It just doesn't sound relaxing." Holding my hand to my head like the great Carnac, I said, "I predict we'll have two of the kids sleeping in our room once they realize we have a balcony."

"We'll just have to set some boundaries," she said.

Setting boundaries didn't concern me. Holding to them was the problem. Once the grandkids start begging, they're harder to bargain with than a Turkish rug merchant.

I stepped into my office to pray, although I pretty much knew the outcome. On my desk, staring up at me, as if calling my name, lay the Princess Cruise brochure promoting the Panama Canal voyage. I picked it up. I found the info on the Hawaii cruise from San Francisco and grimaced when I realized the Hawaii cruise cost nearly one-third less. No wonder they wanted to go.

Taking a deep breath, I walked next door, hoping to convince my daughter to consider the Canal cruise. Scott was home. Tiff and the kids stood next to him.

"Barnibulous," my son-in-law said, using the name he had coined for me. "Tiff was just talking to me about us taking a trip to Hawaii together. I'm a little reluctant, though. Not sure we have enough saved up yet. What do you know about it?"

Well, so much for the Panama Canal. If they weren't sure they could afford Hawaii, then the Canal was a definite no. Olive and Liam, with imploring eyes, stood next to their parents in the kitchen. The baby, Olin, expressed no opinion either way. "Well, Scotticus," I said, using the nickname I had given him, "I was hoping you guys would consider going to the Panama Canal, but—"

"Could I see the brochure?" Taking one look at the price, Scott laughed and handed it back to me.

"Here's the info on the Hawaiian cruise," I said and returned the brochure to him.

"Can I hang on to this?" Scott laid it on the table. "Tiff and I need to talk about it some more." The kids looked as if someone had licked the red off their candy. I decided to leave the matter in God's hands. If Scott and Tiffany decided to go, Linda and I would tag along as the designated babysitters. After all, we loved our grandchildren and enjoyed spending time with them.

A few days later, Scott, Tiff, and the grandkids came over. "We decided we can do it. I should be getting a bonus check in a few weeks, and Tiff convinced me to use it for a vacation. But now it's all up to you guys."

I sensed all eyes turning toward me, burning into my brain like laser beams. I stammered, "Well, uh ... I guess ... uh ... we'll go, or no one in the family will speak to me for a month." For a moment, I considered the potential silence a benefit but quickly squashed the thought.

Linda and Tiff squealed with delight. Olive and Liam jumped up and down. Olin drooled on his mother's shoulder. I smiled and nodded. It felt good to be the family hero, if only for a moment. Later that night, our older son, Josh, came for dinner and celebrated with us when he heard the news.

I accepted the inevitable. We were going to Hawaii with the family in tow. They would not need to drag me onto the ship, screaming as my heels bounced along the gangplank. I was determined to enjoy it. A few days later, I compared the cabin options on the Princess website and showed Linda my discovery. "Honey, a mini-suite costs only $300 more than a regular balcony. What do you say we stretch a little and do that since we'll be on the ship for fifteen days? Besides, the kids'll be hanging out in our room quite a bit." Linda needed no further enticing. My suggestion was like saying "sic 'em" to a pit bull.

The next few months were a whirlwind of activity. The cruise wasn't until February, but we needed to make our deposit and plan activities and excursions. On YouTube, we viewed videos of our ship, the *Grand Princess*. It was an older ship, built in 1998, but had been recently refurbished.

As the holidays approached, the activity level skyrocketed. Owning a retail store specializing in gift items, Linda and I worked late into the night and awakened early each morning. Christmas is a must-win for every retailer. Failing to produce the bucks in December is the equivalent of striking out in the bottom of the ninth in the seventh game of the World Series with the bases loaded. The consequences can be devastating.

Linda goes hog-wild at Christmas, and seven grandchildren afford her a field ripe with opportunity. A mountain of gifts grew beneath our tree. Whenever Josh's or Tiff's kids visited, they poked and prodded the presents, wondering what lay beneath the wrapping paper. On Christmas Day, those headed for Hawaii discovered a bevy of Hawaii-related treasures: snorkels, masks and fins, along with assorted Hawaiian attire. The promised "We'll give each other the cruise for Christmas" had gone the way of the dodo bird.

Once the new year rolled around, Linda shifted into cruise-prep mode. She packed and repacked; she tried on formal dresses and swimsuits. Our cruise was fast approaching. Despite my earlier resistance, I grew more and more excited.

Sometime toward the middle of January, wedged between the endless political dribble on the news, we heard a report of an outbreak of some deadly disease in China known as the coronavirus. Linda and I turned our heads slowly and made eye contact. We shot each other a look that said, "Don't worry. It ain't gonna happen to us!" Then we changed the channel to view something much more intellectually stimulating—*Last Man Stan*ing.

One Friday morning, over our bowls of oatmeal, Linda turned our conversation in a spiritually philosophical direction. "I have the strangest feeling. There's some reason we're supposed to go on this cruise. I know it's not what we originally planned, but God has some purpose in it. I don't know what it is, but I have zero doubt that something big's gonna happen. I'm sure he'll show us at the right time." Linda has a very strong gift of discernment, and I've learned to value her downloads from God through the years. She's usually right.

As I considered what she said, I was overwhelmed by the strangest sensation. Goose bumps rose on my arms. I didn't fully understand it, but deep in my spirit, I sensed the truth of her words. I paused to take it in. "Yes, Linda. For some weird reason, I have the same feeling." We prayed about it, surrendered it to God, and then went about our day.

In early February, Fox News reported the story of the *Diamon* *Princess*. The ship left Yokohama, Japan, on January 20, and a passenger, who disembarked in Hong Kong, had contracted the coronavirus. As more passengers tested positive, all were confined to their quarters. The ship remained in a circling pattern off the coast of Japan until February 4, at which time the passengers were required to remain in quarantine until February 19.

Linda and I looked at each other. A sister ship with this deadly virus onboard, and the passengers were all stuck in their rooms for two weeks? I'd rather sit on a hot stove for an hour than go through what those poor folks were enduring. A nightmarish thought flitted through my mind. We were sailing in less than a month. Would we be cursed with the same fate? What if ... we had spent thousands of dollars on a vacation and it became a living hell?

We shrugged it off as typical media hype. We had nothing to fear. Those kinds of things only happen to other people. But everywhere we looked, the coronavirus story stared back at us. We couldn't avoid it. But the decision had been made; the money had been spent. We were going to Hawaii, and we were determined to be excited about the trip.

Chapter Three

BOARDING THE
GRAND PRINCESS

Februbruary 21, 2020. We awoke at 6:00 a.m., straightened the house, and said goodbye to our dogs, cats, chickens, and goats. Our friend Zulla, who owns a personal transport business, had offered to take us to the cruise terminal. He displayed amazing patience as we crammed his van to the tip-top with suitcases and kid stuff but still had to hold luggage on our laps.

Zulla learned patience the hard way—in jail. As a teen, Zulla ran with gangs, which ultimately led to his imprisonment. In his cell, he knelt and promised God he would follow Him if his sentence were reduced. God granted his prayer. Unlike many jailhouse conversions, Zulla was true to his word. He began studying the Bible with Virgil, a Mister Rogers clone, who was also the jail minister for the church I pastored. After Zulla's release, Virgil baptized him. Zulla and I spent hundreds of hours together in Bible study, or "chopping it up," as he described it. Hanging out with Zulla greatly increased my street-lingo vocabulary.

Fifteen years later, I still enjoy our discussions. On the way to the cruise terminal, I sat in the front seat of Zulla's van, where we deliberated the life and teachings of C. S. Lewis during the hour-and-a-half drive. Linda and I had never boarded a cruise ship in San Francisco. What a breath of fresh air—avoiding a flight into a port city a day early and fighting jet lag the next day. This time the pre-cruise travel took an hour and a half, door to door.

Port authorities and the *Gran Princess* crew were decked out in protective masks and gloves. No one was taking any chances with the coronavirus after the *Diamon Princess* ordeal. Our family filled out health questionnaires, and then a medical officer interrogated us. Linda and I rolled our eyes at each other, resigning ourselves to the tedious but necessary ordeal.

Even so, in less than an hour, we were on the ship. Rumors circulating among the passengers had projected that the process would take three or four hours—the first of a multitude of baseless rumors we encountered on our voyage.

Our rooms weren't ready, so our family headed to the buffet, which Linda and I affectionately dubbed The Trough. The kids took meager portions and picked at their food. But when Scott announced it was time for dessert, their appetites underwent an immediate resurrection. The kids' plates overflowed with enough sugar-laden foods to feed half a dozen beehives for a month.

In the midst of the gluttonizing, Liam announced he needed to use the restroom. I was eager to walk around, so I volunteered to take him. Despite his protests—he insisted that his mom needed to take him—my grandson and I arrived at the men's room without incident. As we headed back to The Trough, Liam decided he needed to go number two. As patiently as a cat stalking prey, I turned back and ushered him into the stall where he could take care of necessary business. As I waited for him to finish, he serenaded me with the "Poop Song," which he had discovered on YouTube and creatively adapted.

Liam's fascination with poop was not unexpected. In fact, six-year-old Liam is obsessed with poop. Much of his free time is consumed with creating new ways for describing and singing about this biological function. Gary Chapman's book, *The Five Love Languages*, actually falls a bit short. Liam's primary love language is "poop talk." Each time I walk through his door, he greets me with an enthusiastic "Hey, Poop Head" or "Poop Face" or "Poop Breath," depending on his mood that particular day. I think his parents rather enjoy the poop labels he has coined for me.

Linda and I made our way back to our room, put away our belongings, and settled in for a nap. We soon heard a knock on our door. Two small voices announced the presence of Olive and Liam. "Mimi, Pa. Can we come in?" Stirred from our slumber, we arose and they entered. Confident this was the first of many intrusions, I reminded myself of how many people would trade places with me for the opportunity to cruise with their grandchildren.

A few hours later, the event we had eagerly anticipated, everyone's favorite moment on any cruise, was announced ... the emergency shipwreck drill. Making our way to the Traveler's Lounge, we squeezed in next to some folks from Canada. One-year-old Olin grew restless. In reality, he was only acting out what we all felt. Except that it isn't cool for adults to fuss and throw fits. His antics provided some comedy relief for the passengers around us.

After Linda and I returned to our cabin, we sat on our deck and observed the skyline of The City. Although we had enjoyed similar views a thousand times, the panorama seemed more beautiful from a cruise ship. Around five o'clock, we strode up to the top deck, so we could observe our sail-away. Linda texted our friend Dave, who pilots the Golden Gate Ferry from Larkspur to San Francisco. He sounded his horn as he sailed by. We waved enthusiastically, but from his vantage point, we must have looked like ants.

As the *Gran⬩ Princess* pulled away from the dock, the passengers onboard were as exuberant as a winning Super Bowl team's fan base. *The Love Boat* theme sounded as we sailed beneath the

Golden Gate Bridge. Surely, nothing could spoil our cruise.

That night, before drifting into the land of nod, I thanked God for all His overwhelming blessings. Lying next to my beautiful wife, my daughter and her family across the hall, all of us on a cruise to Hawaii. I couldn't imagine life being better—truly this was a taste of heaven. Closing my eyes, I recalled the excitement we all felt as we boarded the ship a few hours earlier, especially the delight on the grandkids' faces. I savored the memory, sipping it like a fine wine.

For me, few experiences in life compare with the moment I board a cruise ship. Stress evaporates like vapor from a teakettle. I relish the days of pampering that lie ahead: going to bed when I want, waking up when I feel like it, returning to a clean room each morning and evening, and having a staff of servants to attend to my every whim. Not a bad life at all!

All the preparation and all the expenses were behind us as our family walked up the gangplank that day. The adults' moods were festive; the kids' faces reflected their excitement. We were headed to Hawaii, and we all expected our vacation would be as close to perfect as possible.

Chapter Four

OUR FIRST DAY AT SEA

F ebruary 22, 2020. I blinked and rolled over. No alarm disrupted my slumber. No urgent meetings beckoned me, no phone calls or texts or emails demanded an answer—just the peaceful lapping of waves against the ship and the gentle rocking of our boat as it maneuvered through the ocean. We had no place we had to be, and nothing we had to do.

Eventually I arose, threw on some clothes, and made my way up to The Trough to grab some coffee for Linda. One of my greatest joys in life is bringing my wife coffee in bed each morning and knowing how much she appreciates it. Although room service would have gladly delivered coffee to our door, we both preferred the freedom to awaken when our bodies dictated, undisturbed by a not-so-gentle knock and a voice in broken English announcing, "Room Service."

An hour or so later, we visited The Trough for breakfast and then strolled around the ship. This was our tenth cruise (all with Princess), so we were fairly familiar with the layout of the ship. We ventured toward the swimming pools, where we discovered our grandkids joyously splashing. Their parents appeared a bit less enthusiastic as they supervised the children's aquatic adventures. We hurried away lest we felt the pressure to step into our role as designated babysitters.

We passed the lounges and restaurants, heard the constant ring of slot machines in the casino. All of them beckoned us to exhaust our onboard credits. We located the Jacuzzis, sauna, and other lounge areas. Wandering the decks, I made mental notes of the unexplored spaces we encountered, all promising enjoyment over the next fifteen days.

This cruise was the longest we had taken, and we would

spend nine days at sea. We weren't quite sure about the sea days; the open Pacific could get rough at times. But we were up for the adventure. Sure enough, there was a bit of rocking. Watching others walk was a hoot; they wobbled like drunkards. We, of course, maintained our stability and walked a straight line at all times—although I could never quite understand why folks giggled as we walked toward them.

By the time we returned to our cabin, Scott and Tiffany were approaching us, with Olin in tow. "Where are Olive and Liam?" Linda asked.

"We took them to Discovery Club," Tiff replied. Discovery Club was a supervised area designated for kids to hang out and play. Frankly, I was surprised they had waited so long to deposit the youngsters in this haven of parental rest. Olin reached for us, so Linda and I hurried to our room for a nap, promising to watch him in some vague future time known as "a little later."

Following our nap, we crossed the hall and gently tapped on Tiff's door. Scott answered, looking as though he had endured a covered-wagon journey on the Oregon Trail. Evidently, Olin had awakened everyone in the cabin at 4:00 a.m. The kids had fallen back asleep, but not wanting to risk Olin arousing other passengers, Scott had placed him in a backpack and walked throughout the ship before Olin finally fell back asleep for twenty minutes. Tiffany was feeling seasick, so I gladly offered to take Olin for them, knowing Linda would bear the brunt of the task. Always the thoughtful grandpa.

Shortly thereafter, Olin fell asleep. We laid him on our bed, and I sat on the deck reading C. S. Lewis's *Out of the Silent Planet*, while Linda devoured *Redeeming Love*, written by our good friend, Francine Rivers. What a life!

Tiffany came over about the time Olin began stirring, appearing as if she too had ventured cross-country via Conestoga wagon. "Thanks for watching little Olin. I don't know what we're gonna do if he keeps waking up early. It's hard because he wakes up the other two."

Linda shot a glance my way. Not wanting to be voted the Attila the Hun of grandfathers, I nodded back at her. After forty-six years of marriage, we could read each other's minds.

I determined to take the moral high ground before Linda responded, thus scoring points with my daughter in the Parent Game. "Sweetie, why don't you let the other two sleep over here tonight, so you don't have to worry about it?"

"Really?" she said. "That would be wonderful! Are you sure?"

I hesitated and considered being candidly honest. Instead, I chose a rare moment of wisdom and answered, "Of course. We'd love to give you guys a break. We'll have a movie night with the kids." Even as the words left my lips, I was struck by the reality that the cinematic tastes of young children and adults were as different as a raw onion and a ripe banana. But Tiffany and Scott needed our help, and we stood ready to assist. We would enjoy the evening, although I wondered if this arrangement would continue throughout the remainder of the voyage.

That night was our first formal night. In today's world, we don't get much opportunity to dress up in formal attire. When the Essig family came to our room, Olive glowed with excitement in her formal red dress. Liam was decked out in suit and tie, appropriately sporting Converse high tops as his formal shoes. His fashion statement clearly indicated he was going for a James Bond meets Michael Jordan look. Olin was spruced up in a tie as well, which he ripped off before we got to the elevator.

The formal dinner felt a bit as if we were living in a *Downton Abbey* episode, with stewards and waiters to serve us as we dined on fine food and discussed trivial matters. And the best part? Walking away at the end of the meal without having to worry about paying.

During dinner, Olive was in true Queen-Bee mode. Linda and I gave her that nickname because her goal in life is to rule the universe, and she's wired to do it. She challenged her mom on most of her food choices and insisted on consuming two desserts. Olin fussed for much of the meal, and Tiffany didn't taste a bite of her food until it was cold. But that's pretty much everyday life for a mother of three young kids. Perhaps she was beginning to question her decision to bring the children on this "vacation." A trip to the House of Horrors would probably have been more relaxing.

Following dinner that evening, the two older kids were deposited at our cabin door. The handoff was quicker than a gunslinger slapping leather. Once inside, the kids fought over which movie to watch. Olive wanted to view *Gi⋅get Goes Hawaiian* since Hawaii was our destination. Liam insisted on something along the lines of *Night of the Living Dea⋅ Meets Zombielan⋅*, although in the midst of the epic verbal exchange about their movie choices, I chose to forget the actual title of Liam's film.

Eventually we settled on *Blue Hawaii*, starring Elvis Presley. For one simple reason. It was the movie that I—their ever-loving, perpetually unselfish grandfather—wanted to watch. Olive and Liam settled into the hide-a-bed, and ten minutes into the film, passed out. I collapsed into the bed, flipped off the telly, and fell asleep. So ended our first day at sea.

Chapter Five

LIFE ABOARD THE
GRAND PRINCESS

Febuary 23–25, 2020. Ah, the excitement of days at sea. Step onto your balcony and watch the water roll past the ship. Return later to discover ... more water moving past the ship. Come back again and ... well, you get my point.

Actually, during the days at sea, Linda and I fell into a sweet routine. Awaken whenever we felt like it. Make a coffee run. Drink coffee in bed. Read our Bibles and discuss what we read. Pray together. Head up to breakfast. After breakfast, come back and sit on our deck. Read for a couple of hours. Walk around the promenade deck. Come back to the room and take a nap. Go to The Trough for lunch. Give Scott and Tiff a break from the kids. Take the kids swimming, then take them back to their parents. Return to our room and read, watch a movie, or take a nap. Shower and get dressed for dinner. Dinner in the dining room. Go to a show. Fall asleep, and begin the process all over the next day. Relaxation and enjoyment can really wear a person out.

Days at sea furnished us with loads of time to rest, but after four in a row, I wondered if we'd ever touch terra firma again. Several times I stood on our deck and scanned the horizon for land. Fortunately, I didn't spot any. Otherwise, I may have instinctively shouted, "Land ho," which would have embarrassed Linda almost as much as me wearing pajamas to dinner on a formal night.

One morning on our walk, we strode through Club 21. We were delighted to discover three couples huddled around a table, ready to begin a Bible study—not something we generally encounter on a cruise. Linda and I introduced ourselves. The couples were from diverse parts of the country. We were unable to join the study, since we had committed to babysit, but we talked and prayed with the group.

They asked what Linda and I did vocationally. I explained that I'm a semi-retired pastor, working with Crossing the Jordan, a Christ-based life transformation academy, rescuing those who wish to escape from addiction, sex trafficking, and domestic violence. "It's the most rewarding work of God I've ever experienced—to witness such life-altering transformation occur right before my eyes—even when it breaks my heart to hear their stories of childhood abuse." Linda then described her retail store, the Bird's Nest, which was first located in the town of Bodega, where Alfred Hitchcock filmed *The Bir*•*s*—hence the name Bird's Nest.

What a blessing to be part of God's family—to travel anywhere in the world and find brothers and sisters who love you even though you just met. Those folks were strangers, but they shared our purpose and passion to follow God. Sometimes conversing with strangers can be better than fellowshipping with your church family. After all, you don't hang out with them long enough to discover their "uniqueness" (aka human weirdness). And I possess a great weirdness detector. I just look in the mirror, and see a real weirdo staring back at me!

The most negative part about our sea days was the weather. We had packed for a vacation to Hawaii; we should have planned for a trip to Alaska. After a warm, sunny sail-away in San Francisco, the weather became cold, windy, and rainy for the four days at sea. Each day we bundled up like Eskimos and trekked around the deck. Occasionally, Linda and I wondered aloud if the inclement weather wasn't some sort of foreshadowing of things to come.

Besides the weather, our most challenging situation was dinner—not that the food was bad. It was good. Too good. The choices were downright cruel. How could I decide whether to order filet mignon, chicken cordon bleu, or lobster? And then the dessert menu was shoved in front of us. I had to try everything on the menu, just so I could decide what to order. We were truly enduring a spiritual test of gargantuan proportion. Certainly not on the level of Christians in North Korea ... but a test, nonetheless. Okay... honestly, it wasn't much of a test at all.

After a couple of evenings in the dining room, I observed a strange phenomenon as our family was seated. Several servers huddled together, pointing in our direction, each shaking his head. Some even feigned stabbing themselves with steak knives. Perhaps it was the fact that each family member possessed unique dining quirks. Olin drops more food on the floor than he eats and even throws some at adjoining tables. Liam wants only cheeseburgers with catsup and refuses to touch the burger if it's prepared any other way. Olive believes she possesses the power to perceive what's best for each person to eat, so she attempts to order for everyone. Linda doesn't eat white flour or sugar. Tiffany orders everything on the side. Scott orders multiple items of each course. And I have a hard time deciding what to order. Okay, I'm exaggerating. The waiters were amazing and didn't mind serving us at all. But I must say, the Cargiles and Essigs are quirky eaters.

During those four days, I also found time to write. Lugging my computer to the back of the ship, I sequestered myself at a corner table. For the past ten years, I've written an encouraging weekly devotion, "Barney's Bullet," which I place on my website, BarneyCargile.com. On the cruise, I labored to convert those articles into a book. Linda spent her time reading and painting with watercolors. No, actually that's not totally true. Most of her time was consumed with utilizing her phone. Besides sending pictures and texts to friends, she attempted to squeeze every possible bit of daily news data out of her device.

For some odd reason, Linda and I both continued to strongly sense that we were destined to be on this cruise, which made no sense to either of us. We wouldn't have chosen this Hawaiian island-hopping cruise, although we felt extremely blessed to be onboard. But, from the moment Tiffany approached us about traveling with them, we both were filled with a weird sensation that God had something significant for us to do on this vacation. We mentioned the feeling to each other on almost a daily basis.

Every evening following dinner, the family returned to our cabins and found heart-shaped chocolates on each pillow. We convinced the children that the "cruise elves" deposited them there for good little boys and girls. That tale may have worked except, as they changed for the evening, their mother removed the sugar-laden treat. She was convinced that consuming one more gram of glucose could potentially skyrocket their glycemic levels through the stratosphere.

One night after dinner, she wasn't quite quick enough. Looking around, she discovered baby Olin with brown drool running down his chops. Her suspicions were confirmed the next day when tiny bits of red foil appeared in his diaper.

Like a well-oiled machine, Linda and I developed an effective routine with the two older kids. Rather than a classic battle each evening over movie choices, we set up a rotation system: Olive chose the movie one night, then Liam picked the movie the next night. They had their own TV to enjoy on the hide-a-bed, so Linda and I could watch whatever we wanted on the other TV. But one night, we all piled into the big bed and watched *Grease*. Linda and I hadn't seen it in years. I knew some inappropriate spots appeared in the film, but after much theological musing, determined neither child would apostatize from the faith as a result.

I'm in the season of life where subtitles greatly enhance my viewing. As much as the words on the screen annoy my family, they allow it because otherwise I'd be asking, "What did they say?" every two minutes. Then "Greased Lightning," Liam's favorite song from the movie, came on. I guess I had never understood the words to the song, but when I saw them on the screen, let's just say I was glad Liam couldn't read. I wouldn't have been comfortable answering the questions the lyrics might raise in a six-year-old's mind.

Each afternoon, as we prepared for dinner, we watched the Fox News channel. More and more coverage was devoted to the coronavirus. The newscasters described the conditions of the unfortunate folks aboard the *Diamon Princess*, who were confined in quarantine off the coast of Japan. I couldn't imagine how brutal that would be! I prayed and thanked God that he had spared us from that fate.

Chapter Six

ISLAND HOPPING

February 26–29, 2020. I slid out of bed and squeezed past Liam and Olive's couch—not daring to bump it, lest I disturb their nocturnal dormancy and unleash the bliss of grouchy kids in the early morn. I opened the door onto our deck and stepped outside. The breeze was warm, and I inhaled its fragrance. Then I saw it. Small but unmistakable. Land. The Garden Island, Kauai. I stepped inside and motioned for Linda to come outside. Sleepily, she followed.

After breakfast, we returned and watched from our deck as the beauty of the island unfolded. It glowed like an emerald reflecting the sun. Once the ship docked, Tiff's family headed ashore, loaded down with masks, snorkels, and fins. I counted my blessings—they were going ashore without Linda and me. Looking down from our deck, we waved at the Essigs as they departed. Olive and Liam attempted WWF moves on each other as they waited in line. For some odd reason, the other passengers gave the family a wide expanse as they walked past. Thank God, Linda and I had booked an excursion.

At the appropriate time, we disembarked. Climbing into a bus, we headed to our destination, the Wailua River. Apparently, much of *Blue Hawaii* was filmed on Kauai. Every couple of minutes our bus driver connected what we could see out our window with the movie. "This was the waterfall in Blue Hawaii. This was the beach used in Blue Hawaii. This was the hotel where Elvis stayed while filming *Blue Hawaii*. Elvis ate a coconut from this tree while filming ..."

As we boarded the small flat-bottomed boat designed for our river cruise, our host welcomed us. He held a ukulele, and I hoped he didn't plan on singing to us. But the evidence suggested otherwise. As soon as we pulled away from the dock, an entire band joined him, serenading us with cornball Hawaiian songs. Actually, I rather enjoyed them, but I pretended I didn't like them for Linda's sake, who rolled her eyes and complained under her breath nonstop. I considered yelling out some requests just to bug her. Fortunately, my good sense prevailed. We sat back and took it in. The scenery on each side of the boat beckoned us, like a baby reaching for her mother.

We arrived at our destination, the Fern Grotto—a cave entrance where hundreds of ferns hang upside down. Amazing. In all our travels, we had never seen anything like it. And yes, our guide was quick to point out this was the backdrop for the wedding scene in (take a guess) ... *Blue Hawaii.*

As the bus pulled into the cruise dock, our driver sang the worst rendition of "Aloha 'Oe" ("Farewell to Thee") in the history of music. Thankfully, I don't think he realized how terrible he sounded. His voice brought tears to our eyes, but not for the appropriate reasons. I would've thrown money at him, hoping he would stop, but he probably would have interpreted it as encouragement to sing an encore. What he lacked in vocal ability, he more than made up for with a kind heart. I guess the song was his way of showing appreciation. I can only say that his singing took a lot of courage. So ended our first day of island hopping on beautiful Kauai.

The next day we docked in Honolulu. Early that morning Linda informed me that I would not be going ashore. Actually, she told me she would not be going ashore. I was free to do as I wished. I think she knew going ashore alone wouldn't be much fun, so I stayed onboard and discovered we would be babysitting

Olive and Liam. "Scott and Tiff need a break from them," Linda informed me. Having just spent six days with our grandkids, I could feel their parents' need to escape for a little mommy and daddy time.

Most passengers considered Honolulu their number-one destination. But having been there, Linda and I, for the most part, deemed it just a big city. Beautiful, yes, but a huge city nonetheless. We thoroughly enjoyed our day with the grandkids. Since the ship was nearly empty, we came and went as we pleased. We allowed the kids to eat extra desserts, then took them up to deck 17, which gave us a bird's-eye view of the skyline as we all soaked in the large hot tubs.

On February 28, we docked in Lahaina, Maui. This turned out to be the best day of the trip. Lahaina is a nostalgic place for our family. Linda and I had visited Lahaina on our previous two trips to Hawaii, the first in early 1975. A few months after marrying in 1973, Linda and I purchased a purebred Afghan hound. We bred her nearly two years later, sold the pups, took the money, and ran off to Maui for two weeks. It was a honeymoon of sorts for us because we couldn't afford a honeymoon following our wedding. In 1994, we took both our children, Josh and Tiffany, to Hawaii and stayed near Lahaina again.

I couldn't help but take a sentimental journey as I pondered how much our family had grown through the years—two on our first trip, four on our second visit, and now seven. And that didn't include Josh and his four children.

As Linda and I walked through old Lahaina with Tiff's family, we reminisced about what we did on previous visits—like the time I nearly got my ear bitten off by a macaw, which was positioned on my shoulder while the family posed for a picture in 1994. The bird's owner assured us that the bird had never bitten anyone before. Right. Tiff suggested we get another family photo. You can imagine how well that suggestion landed on yours truly.

Scott and I purchased round-trip city bus passes for the family. We hopped on a bus and headed off to Whaler's Village, a popular spot, loaded with shops and restaurants. Linda and I spent a lot of days there in 1975, just hanging out and doing nothing. Like most things in life, the village didn't look the same. Of course, neither do Linda or I. Our favorite restaurant was still in operation, but we opted for fish tacos to go.

We took our feast to the beach for a picnic. I read and napped, while everyone else swam and snorkeled. Little Olin took his mouthful of taco, threw it on the sand, then picked it up and swallowed the sandy snack. I'll bet that wreaked havoc on his intestinal track.

After a few hours, we walked back to the entrance of Whalers Village from the beach. We paused at the sperm whale's skeleton, hanging overhead. Linda and I had our picture taken at that spot in 1975. We asked a stranger to snap a shot of us forty-five years later, and then a pic of the whole family. "Time passes quickly" is a timeworn cliché, but that visit to Lahaina reminded me of how rapidly the years pass and how much life changes us.

We hopped off the city bus at the edge of Old Town Lahaina and strolled back to the ship, looking in the shops. Liam and I stopped at Whaler's Locker, a self-proclaimed shark museum. We marveled at the size of all the shark jaws on display. His awe gave me a bit of leverage, as I was able to threaten the lad with feeding him to the sharks the next time he misbehaved. Needless to say, he shrugged off my idle threats.

However, his interest in these aquatic giants stirred a stimulating zoological discussion between the two of us—actually more of a monologue on Liam's part. All the way through town and even as we boarded the ship, my six-year-old grandson provided me with nonstop biological information concerning tiger sharks, great whites and megalodons. His informative lecture then turned toward which of these would win in a battle, with the megalodon emerging as the ultimate winner. From there, his dissertation evolved into a battle between land creatures: buffaloes, hippos, and the T. rex. Then he introduced the ultimate land creature ... Godzilla. I purposely chose to withhold the detail that Godzilla was fictional, lest I furnish the lad with further fuel for discussion.

The experience reminded me of an argument that occurred several years back between my two oldest grandsons, Jeb and Oliver, over another earth-shattering concern—the best way to kill zombies. A baseball bat, shotgun, chainsaw? They almost came to fisticuffs over the issue. It's amazing how passionate we become over matters that will never occur (like many church issues). At least Liam's fervent discourse contained some basis of factual information.

Fortunately, we reached our room before any further epic zoological battles arose. My brain was on the verge of exploding from information overload. I shut the door and collapsed until dinner. It had been an exhausting but wonderful day.

The final leg of our adventures was the Big Island, Hawaii. Prior to the trip, I had visions of visiting the volcano. But the volcano excursion was expensive, the weather was rainy, and we were exhausted. Option two was to connect with our friends Steve and Karen who were training at a YWAM (Youth With A Mission) base at Kona. That, however, required that we rent a car and drive a couple of hours each way. If the slightest problem occurred and we arrived late, the ship would leave without us. Since booking a flight home and missing the remainder of a cruise we had paid for didn't appeal to me, Linda and I opted out. Instead, we stayed onboard and rested. I'm sure we missed a great opportunity, but vacations should be relaxing. When you find you're forcing yourself to have fun, the vacation ceases to be fun.

Linda and I concluded the best way to enjoy Hawaii is to choose one island as a vacation spot because island hopping wasn't a relaxing experience. For us, cruises are the best vacation for value, service, and overall experience. Except for Hawaii. The Lord tested my self-control in this matter. I engaged in intense spiritual warfare to make certain I didn't remind Linda that island hopping was one of my initial concerns about cruising to Hawaii. And, most important, I stopped myself from saying those four deadly words, "I told you so."

Chapter Seven

HOMEWARD BOUND

March 1–4. Back at sea again for four more days. No complaints, other than the weather, which remained cold and stormy. Each morning we stood on our decks until the frigid "tropical" air forced us inside, shivering.

Our routine continued, just as it had on the four sea days en route to the islands. We were on a cruise with our family, being served anything we wanted, whenever we wanted it, and basically doing whatever we wanted. Following the sea days, we would stop at Ensenada. Another sea day would follow, and then on March 7, we would wake up in San Francisco. Zulla would meet us, and we would return to our castle. The whole family relaxed, secure in our plans.

As much as we were enjoying the cruise, we had many plans once we arrived home and resumed our normal routine. Except for my first two trips to India, no one in the family had ever been away from home this long.

Our granddaughter Kylie was housesitting. Linda and I used the free internet on the ship and called her regularly to make certain all our animals were alive and no one had burned our place down. Linda missed her goats, sheep, dogs, cats, chickens, geese, and ducks. (Did I mention she's an animal lover?) She also grieved the missed opportunity of seeing her roses bloom: "By the time we get home, the bushes will all have blossomed."

Tiffany spoke regularly of her fortieth birthday party on March 14, which two of her friends were hosting one week after we returned. St Patrick's Day would occur three days later. Being half Irish, Linda had never missed the family tradition of eating corned beef and cabbage on March 17. As part of the celebration, I usually related the story of St. Pattie's life or read a portion of his writings. Linda loves celebrating holidays family-style and was making plans for Easter a few weeks after we returned. Josh's family would join us too. The thought of returning home brought us more peace than the Geneva Convention.

Then everything changed. On Tuesday, March 3, a familiar British voice droned over the P.A. in our suite just as we headed up to The Trough for breakfast. "Good morning, ladies and gentlemen. This is your captain speaking." I tuned him out. Each morning he bored us with a deluge of technical information, spelling out the latitude and longitude we were approaching, how many sea miles we had covered, and yada, yada, yada—much like Charlie Brown's teacher. Only this time, he didn't.

"I have an important announcement."

Well, well, I thought. This could be interesting. As it turned out, "interesting" didn't begin to describe what unfolded. Referring to the next phase of our journey as "interesting" would be like calling the Grand Canyon "a big ditch."

The captain continued. "A passenger on our previous voyage has developed coronavirus. Since our entire crew and sixty-nine passengers were on that cruise with him, they will all be tested for the virus. The US Coastguard has already arranged for test kits to be flown in by helicopter, which should be happening in a few hours. Until the results of these tests are known, we encourage you all to maintain minimum contact with other passengers."

Okay, I thought. Let's hope nobody has it. But, in the overall scheme of things, it doesn't sound like that big of a deal. I'm sure no one's gonna test positive. Let me just go get my breakfast. Linda's already telling me I'm getting grouchy.

The captain paused, then added, "Because of this, we are

re-routing our cruise and will not be stopping in Ensenada. Instead, we will be going directly to San Francisco. We apologize for this inconvenience. We will keep you informed of any other changes."

It was hard to imagine, but somewhere on the ship, some poor sucker was probably cursing the captain because that particular passenger had his heart set on stopping in Ensenada. But not me. I'd been to Ensenada a couple of times, and let's just say it isn't exactly the garden of Eden.

Linda and I looked at each other, shrugged, crossed the hall to Scott and Tiff's room, and knocked. They were headed to breakfast as well. We boarded the elevator and entered The Trough. Like always, we scrubbed our hands at the washing station. After getting our food and settling into a booth, I asked, "So what do y'all think about this? Disappointed we're not going to Ensenada?"

Both adults snorted. Then Tiffany added, "I'm excited that we'll probably be getting home a day or so early, which is great with us. We're both ready to get home."

Scott added, "Yeah, after nearly two weeks with the kids on the cruise, it might be a good thing."

I looked at Liam trying to shove an entire waffle down Olin's mouth and instantly understood.

"I'm really looking forward to working in the garden," Tiff added. She is the family's organic gardener. Like my mom, she loves getting in the dirt—planting, growing, and harvesting vegetables. In addition, she grocery shops for the family and cooks dinner. Linda and I play the all-important unselfish role of consuming whatever she cooks. It's a huge sacrifice, but we're always up for the challenge.

We all agreed it would be good to get off the ship a day or two early. "I can't see any way they're gonna keep us on the ship," I said. "I mean, what're they gonna do? Confine us to our cabins for a week?" Everyone got a good laugh out of that. But as the words left my lips, I recalled the unfortunate passengers of the *Diamon♦ Princess*. That was different, though. No one on our ship had the virus.

For the next two days, passengers droned on about the captain's announcement. Few seemed heartbroken about missing Ensenada, but, at the same time, a low-grade fear grew among the masses onboard. What if the test results came back positive? What would happen? Could some of us be infected?

Since I possess a weird sense of humor (which has plagued me since childhood), I attempted to lighten the mood onboard. On one occasion, I stepped into a crowded elevator. After the door closed, I said, "I don't suppose anyone would think it was funny if I started violently coughing right now." Most everyone laughed, but a few folks instinctively moved to the opposite corner of the elevator.

A couple of hours later, I headed to my writing spot in a booth at the back of the boat. Shortly thereafter, a hubbub arose nearby. I peeked out the window. In the distance, a helicopter approached our ship. I phoned Linda, and she rushed up just as the chopper circled the *Gran♦ Princess*. The coronavirus test kits had arrived.

When Linda and I returned to our cabin and turned on Fox News, we saw video footage of what we had just witnessed firsthand. In fact, our cruise had become the lead story on all the networks. I felt as if we had become unwilling participants in a reality-TV show.

For the remainder of the day and into the next, our vessel reverberated with conversations and questions about the coronavirus. Rumors flew faster than a supersonic jet. One disturbing bit of gossip had something to do with being shipped off to an underground isolation facility in Kansas for a month until we were cleared to enter mainstream society (or at least something to that effect). I suppose when a dearth of knowledge exists, human nature tends to move into the arena of worst-case scenarios. Periodically, the captain briefed us with updates, but his announcements weren't exactly chock-full of information. "We have nothing new to report" was the repetitive cry. These disclosures heightened the passengers' stress level. The timeworn phrase "no news is good news" didn't cut it.

Most of us sat glued to the television, devouring any tidbits of information. Gradually, we realized that, in some cases, the media received updates before the captain did. Hence, he was unable to disseminate data to us in a timely manner, elevating the frustration among some passengers. Eavesdropping on conversations around the ship only created more confusion—the verbiage consisted of pooled ignorance. Some folks were concerned they might be required to remain on the ship for a month. Others were fearful they might test positive. Many shrugged the virus off as nothing and were angry over the disruption. But everywhere we turned it was the continual topic of conversation.

Emotions ran the gamut from anger to terror to acceptance of our circumstances. The level of victimhood and entitlement among our fellow passengers amazed us: complaining about how much this inconvenience had "wrecked my trip" or whining that the quality of service had deteriorated. Others were convinced the cruise line had caused the disaster by neglecting to take the necessary precautions to prevent it.

Our family made it our mission to counter this negativity with words of gratitude and encouragement. In restaurants, elevators and lounges, we mentioned how thankful we were to be on a ship, rather than under quarantine in some austere environment. Linda reminded everyone she encountered that it would all work out for good and soon be over and we would all be home shortly. Everything would then be right with the world once again.

Chapter Eight

THE NEWS ONLY GETS BETTER

Marst 5. In life, a handful of events occur that are burned into people's memories. They remember where they were and what they were doing when they received the life-altering news: the Twin Towers falling on 9/11, the space shuttle exploding, JFK's death. I never tired of hearing my dad share his memories of Pearl Harbor Day. He was at the movies on Sunday afternoon, December 7, 1941, at a small theater in the tiny West Texas town of Rising Star. The movie was interrupted to announce the news, then the film continued. But none of the patrons present that day would ever be the same.

What we experienced on the *Grand Princess* doesn't begin to compare to the tragic news of Pearl Harbor being bombed, but I'll never forget it anyway. Since we only had a couple of days left on the cruise, we decided to enjoy a formal lunch in the Da Vinci restaurant. The time was nearing 1:30 p.m. I had almost finished my steak-and-kidney pie and was debating whether to order dessert. I had pretty much determined to pass on it because we would enjoy a formal dinner in the dining room in a few hours.

Once again, the captain's familiar voice boomed over the intercom and disturbed our culinary delight. "Ladies and gentlemen, this is your captain. We have received back the coronavirus test results." The restaurant grew silent. The captain paused, as if for dramatic effect, before he continued. "Of the crew members and passengers who were tested ... twenty-one tested positive—nineteen crew members and two passengers. They will remain in isolation until we return to port."

I scanned the restaurant. His announcement had stunned the crowd. "We are asking all passengers to take extra measures to protect themselves," he said. "Wash your hands frequently, and maintain a safe distance of at least six feet between yourself and other passengers."

A communal chuckle from our fellow diners swept through the Da Vinci restaurant, as if to say, "Good luck with that."

"We are also asking passengers to avoid crowded areas. For your protection, we have canceled ..." The captain then rattled off a litany of scheduled events that had been eliminated. I listened closely and concluded we would not be missing anything of significance. Apparently, we had escaped unscathed from the shipboard virus scare. I speared the last remaining morsels on my plate.

But the captain wasn't finished. He paused for a few moments, then dropped a verbal hand grenade. "All passengers are also confined to your quarters for the remainder of the voyage. Please return to your cabins as quickly as possible." Click!

The communal chuckle that had moved through the dining room a few moments earlier transformed into a communal groan. The captain's strategy amazed me. Rather than taking a straightforward approach at the beginning of his announcement, he related a montage of irrelevant information before dropping the bomb on us. Who cares if we need to maintain a safe distance from other passengers? Who cares if the shows had been canceled? None of us could attend anyway because we'd all be locked away in our stinking cabins. I can only suppose he was attempting to soften the blow. It didn't work.

A few passengers stood and departed. Some were noticeably angry. I called for our server and ordered crème brûlée, realizing my days of indulging my palate with sweet delights were at an end. At the time it seemed a tragedy of immense proportion

After finishing my dessert, Linda and I left the dining room. I wish I could say we followed the captain's instructions and rushed back to our cabin. But truth be told, giant tortoises could have beaten us back to our suite. We were going to be locked up in that small space for several days. Why get there sooner than absolutely necessary? Arriving in our room, I filled a suitcase with dirty laundry. Linda and I had planned to wash clothes right after lunch anyway. She interrupted my foolish venture. "What are you doing?"

"Well, we were going to do laundry. I better get it done now. We won't have much of a chance after this. Besides, I'm down to my last pair of clean underwear."

"Didn't you hear the captain? We have to stay in our room."

"Aww, they won't care. It'll just take a minute."

"It'll take an hour. And I do think they'll care. Look down the hall."

I opened the door and scanned the hallway. Room stewards were coming and going like ants on a hill, preparing for the additional workload of an already overwhelmingly busy schedule. At that point, the reality of the captain's announcement hit me like a Nolan Ryan fastball to the head. We really wouldn't be leaving our cabin for several days. I resigned myself to rinsing out my socks and underwear in the suite's tiny bathroom sink. As for my other garments, I could air them out and wear them dirty for the remainder of the voyage. No problem for me, but I wasn't so sure the rest of the family would appreciate my non-hygienic attire.

A gentle rap on our door a short time later stirred me from a nap. Our room steward, Arnold, decked out in a mask and latex gloves, stepped back when I opened door. He sat two papers on the floor of the hallway, containing our menus for the next twenty-four hours. We actually had a couple of decent options. We each filled out a menu, then slid the two papers under our door into the hallway. I assumed that would remain standard operational procedure for the remainder of the voyage.

A short time later, another rap—only it wasn't so gentle. Opening the door, Scott, Tiff, and the kids were sneaking over from across the hall. The adults had a far-off dazed look in their eyes and mumbled somewhat incoherently, "We need a break ... need a break. Is it okay if we invade your cabin? We'll kill each other if we all have to stay one more minute in that tiny inside room."

Olive and Liam were performing what appeared to be a re-enactment of *The Three Stooges*—Moe poking Curly in the eye. For the sake of the parents' sanity, Linda and I permitted the invasion. Stepping aside, I waved them in. Olive and Liam were already sleeping on our sofa bed anyway. Hopefully, the stewards would overlook our transgression. After all, we were traveling as a family, and I was confident the ordeal would all be over in a day or two.

Chapter Nine

CABIN FEVER

arch 5–8. In sixty-six years of life, I'd never experienced anything quite like cruise quarantine. Normally, when we encounter new situations, we have some point of reference to which we compare the situation. But not this time. I searched my memory banks. Nothing. Nada. Zilch. This was new turf for all of us.

During our quarantine, we stayed relatively busy (if you consider binge-watching movies, napping, and snacking "busy"). I attempted to write a bit, but when the kids came over ... well, any grandparent can deduce how that affected my concentration. Attempting to memorize *War an• Peace* in the midst of a stampede would have been easier. Our room became the designated TV room; Scott and Tiff's room was reserved for napping, especially for Olin (although I engaged in my share of horizontal meditation across the hall as well).

Twice a day Tiff led the family in a dance party, which gave us some aerobic exercise. The activity demanded precise coordination to avoid inflicting head injuries to one another. Linda and I grunted through the routine, then collapsed on the bed. We wiggled our toes and told ourselves we were getting a great workout.

In between all the events in our busy social schedule, Linda managed to help the kids create gratitude pictures, portraying specific aspects of life for which they were thankful. Early on, we discovered that the best way to avoid negativity was to maintain a grateful heart. Access to a mini-suite with a balcony turned out to be a major blessing. I shudder to think how Scott and Tiff would have fared, stuck in their tiny cabin with three small children. Sure, we were crowded. Sure it was inconvenient. But during the moments I focused on my blessings, surrounded by family, I considered myself a very fortunate man.

Once we were confined to our cabins, we essentially gave up control of our lives. For six days, we were helplessly dependent on others. We couldn't go anywhere or do anything outside our room. In a sense, we were forced to do whatever the captain and crew told us. I developed empathy, on a small scale, for prisoners and POWs, or even those living in nursing homes. Linda and I both gained a deeper appreciation for freedom once it had been taken from us.

Each morning, we received the Princess Patter, a daily bulletin outlining activities of the day. Only now there weren't any activities. It simply gave us coronavirus updates. One of those issues contained news that elicited a "No way!" from each of us, followed by a cheer. Princess Cruise Lines was refunding the entire cost of our cruise. Then the following day, the Princess Patter informed us that each passenger would also receive an additional free cruise in the future.

Besides the refund, the service and the care provided by this amazing cruise line were over the top. They added ninety-nine movie selections for us to view. Each day the kids received activity packets, toys, and stuffed animals. Meals were delivered to our cabin three times daily. We could call room service for a fruit basket, cheese tray, or pot of coffee whenever we wished. The cruise line even provided free alcoholic beverages. Overall, the food was good, but like everything in life, nothing's perfect. The *Gran◆ Princess* staff did the best they could with a difficult situation, but quarantine is still quarantine.

One day, I was stunned beyond words when a newscaster

reported that a group of passengers were filing a lawsuit against the cruise line. In the midst of quarantine, we actually received a phone call from an attorney offering to represent us in a suit against Princess Cruise Line. When Linda informed him that we felt as well cared for as a nursing babe and that we would not be suing the company, he grew angry and argued with her.

After forty-six years of marital bliss, I've learned the futility of that sort of discussion with my little Buttercup. Beauty's ever-so-gentle demeanor can quickly transform into beastly behavior. She unleashed on the attorney. I stood back and enjoyed the heated exchange—a different fool was the target of her fury.

On another newscast, a passenger was quoted as saying, "People are fighting over rotten food." Our whole family laughed. We had more than enough to eat, so no one was fighting, and our food was far from "rotten." Our meals were not Four Seasons quality, but they were more than adequate. "Talk about entitlement," Linda said. Yes, entitlement, ingratitude, and a victim mind-set are blights on our culture and infect many lives ... far worse than the coronavirus.

The captain provided updates several times daily, and the news only grew worse. We would not be allowed to dock in San Francisco, and, at that point, he did not know when or where we would be docking. Our time onboard would obviously be extended. We called Kylie and asked if she could housesit a bit longer. Scott called his boss and let him know he would not be at work on Monday, and I canceled a speaking engagement at a church on Sunday.

Uncertainty plagued us. As humans we like to know what's coming so we can prepare for worst-case scenarios. But God was using our situation to teach us acceptance, gratitude, and living in the moment. Without those disciplines, the what-ifs would have consumed us. We prayed together each day. Linda continued to supervise the kids' daily art projects, specifically creating gratitude pictures. This helped them remain in a state of thankfulness (at least as much as two small children possibly could) and furnished us with the precious gift of silence for a few minutes as they drew.

One evening Scott grabbed his guitar and played worship songs. Tiff sang with him. They often lead worship at our church and harmonize beautifully. Linda and I were moved to tears by the presence of the Holy Spirit in that worship setting. Even little Olin participated in the worship, bobbing and clapping his hands. No matter where we are or what our external circumstances may be, the light of God's presence breaks through the darkness.

If I could choose only one word to label those days of shipboard quarantine, it would be surreal. Turning on the news and seeing our ship as the lead story was weird—the kind of thing you think only happens to "other people." But then something occurred that took our sense of surreal to a whole new level.

Chapter Ten

THE WORD ON THE STREET

March 9. I yawned, stretched, and stared at the clock. 6:00 a.m. I wanted to roll over and sleep some more, but slumber eluded me. For an instant, I thought of going up to The Trough for coffee. Then I remembered—those days had waved goodbye. Immediately, my mind seized on a multitude of questions. Would we dock today? How long after docking would we be allowed to disembark? Where would we stay? How long before we could go home? Would our family be together?

We had been told only that we would be taken to some sort of military facility. In my mind, I pictured a POW-type camp run by a combination of the Gestapo and the KGB. If we were caught smuggling notes to the outside world, we would be shot. Okay, I'm exaggerating. But our thoughts can certainly take us far from reality, if we allow them.

The government didn't know what to do with us, so they placed us in a holding pattern, circling fifty miles off the California coast. In the midst of this uncertainty, the family maintained our determination to make the most of it. Although far from what we desired, we felt blessed. Our situation could have been a whole lot worse than being quarantined on a cruise ship. We weren't in North Korea or Somalia. We were healthy and had plenty of food. Too much, in fact. We watched movies, read books, played games, and, of course, continued our daily family dance parties.

Then Scott received a phone call. A relative of a relative worked for the San Francisco NBC affiliate and had heard Scott was sequestered on the *Gran‣ Princess* with his wife and three small children. The news team wanted to interview Scott. The station especially liked the angle of three young kids cooped up in an inside cabin with their parents. The ultimate human-interest angle. They should have asked me. I was the one cooped up with young kids in my room. Ah, the injustices of life. Anyway, Scott declined, but Tiff said yes. The first interview turned out to be a pebble in a pond.

The following morning the station requested another interview. This time Tiffany declined and told the network to contact me. I agreed. Evidently, the segment went well. They interviewed me, then Linda, then both of us three times, all via FaceTime. Along the way, the local ABC affiliate jumped into the mix with several interviews wedged in between NBC's sessions. Then our local newspaper, the *Santa Rosa Press Democrat* phoned and interviewed me five times while in quarantine. Also, KGO news radio conducted two live on-the-air interviews. On some days, we practically needed a social director to manage our schedule. We certainly weren't sitting around twiddling our thumbs in mind-numbing boredom.

In the midst of this media buzz, *The To▪ay Show* and *Goo▪ Morning America* got wind of our situation and phoned for an interview as well. They felt Linda and I presented ourselves well on camera and wanted us to do a segment on the national news. Although we were nervous, we acted natural, even teasing and joking with each other.

Finally, a Christian news podcast, "The World and Everything in It," contacted me and asked me keep a daily video diary of our experiences. They would air it after we returned home. This podcast, an arm of *Worl▪* news magazine, averages eight million downloads per year and is ranked in the top fifty downloads on iTunes.

As the interviews stacked up, a flurry of texts, emails, Facebook messages, and phone calls from friends around the world poured in. We hadn't heard from some of them in years. We felt as if we had entered *The Twilight Zone*, only it was actual life. Finally, we were beginning to sense God's purpose in placing us on this cruise.

In each interview—TV, radio, newspaper, or podcast—we were upfront about our Christian faith. We talked about the challenges of isolation but always emphasized that God provided the strength we needed for our struggles. We highlighted our joy and gratitude. The media didn't quite know how to handle a family with such positive attitudes. Others who were interviewed whined and complained about how hard it was. That may be the reason the media returned to our family for more and more interviews.

We couldn't ignore the irony. Here we were, confined to our quarters on the open seas and isolated from other human beings, yet God gave us a far-reaching platform so we could share His hope and peace— a larger platform than any we had experienced in all our years of ministry. God has the best sense of humor in the universe, and He loves to surprise us. In the Old Testament, He spoke through a donkey, for goodness' sake. So I guess He can speak through me (although Linda would be the first to say Balaam's ass and I have a lot in common at times).

The six days of confinement in our stateroom merged together—blurry as looking through smeared eyeglasses. On Sunday, March 9, the captain confirmed that we were heading to Oakland. The following day, March 10, we stepped onto our deck and saw the shoreline growing closer.

The elation of seeing land again shot through me like a race-horse at the gate. Home. Passengers crammed onto their decks on the port side of the ship. Cheering erupted from the crowd as we passed under the Golden Gate Bridge. I recorded the celebration on my phone, and later it aired on the local news. I'm confident the free alcohol contributed to the passengers' jovial mood. It felt good to be back in the Bay area. But how long would the euphoria last?

As we moved past Alcatraz, I took a picture of the world's most famous prison and sent it to several friends. "They changed the location of our quarantine facility," I texted. I've learned that if I can't find humor in difficult situations, I'm in a heap of trouble.

All seven members of the family stood on the deck as the crew navigated the ship to the Oakland pier. The sun on our faces and warm breeze in our hair belied the sober nature of our situation. We were back in the Bay area, yes, but what next? I pushed aside the anxious thoughts that arose in my mind. Our family would face those obstacles when we encountered them.

Returning to our cabins, we ate and rested like any other day. But our hearts felt lighter. We were a step closer to going home. Shortly after the ship docked, an official from CDC (Centers for Disease Control and Prevention) stopped at our cabin and informed us that we would be leaving with the Essigs since we were traveling as a family. Later, we were given numbered and colored luggage tags. My tags and Linda's were different colors and numbers than those of Tiff's family. I didn't have to be Sherlock Holmes to deduce we would probably be separated. One more instance of conflicting information.

We were also told all California passengers would be quarantined at Travis Air Force Base, but we still had lots of questions. Would Scott and Tiff's family be with us during those fourteen days? Would Linda and I be together? Would we be drawn and quartered or merely placed on the rack? We prayed that someone would answer our questions soon.

Chapter Eleven

WILL WE EVER GET OFF?

March 10. Later Monday afternoon, our family gathered in our room—where else? —and ho-hummed our way through *Spi⊲erman*. Would Peter Parker escape the clutches of The Green Goblin, or would the movie end differently from the other ninety-nine times we had viewed it? The kids were packed and ready, Olive with her Barbie backpack and Liam toting his rugged Stegosaurus knapsack. The stewards had picked up our luggage earlier. Families were departing first; Scott and Tiff fidgeted nervously, ready to leave the ship. With each announcement over the PA system, we paused, listening as if E. F. Hutton were speaking.

Once more, the captain's British voice interrupted our cinematic experience: "Green three, green three may now disembark."

Tiffany gasped. "That's us! Let's go!" Abandoning *Spi⊲erman* to his fate, we hugged one another and said goodbye. Linda and I assumed we wouldn't be with the Essigs during the fourteen-day quarantine. Their departure was bittersweet. After being together for eighteen days, it seemed strange that we wouldn't see one another for a fortnight.

But the separation was only somewhat bittersweet. As the door closed, I turned off the TV. "Shhh," I whispered. Linda and I closed our eyes and listened. Nothing. The most beautiful sound we had experienced for two and a half weeks. The sound of silence. But ... our reprieve of auditory bliss was short-lived. A few minutes later, that all-too-familiar rap on our door sounded. Linda and I glanced at each other. Could they be back?

I opened the door and there they all stood. I'm thankful we had our clothes on.

"What happened?" Linda asked. I was too grief-stricken to

speak.

"They didn't call *green* three. They called *cream* three," Tiffany said.

My first thought was why hadn't they stayed downstairs and waited for green three to be called. Fortunately, my better judgment prevailed, and I simply asked, "Why would they have two colors that sound so much alike? It's not like there's a shortage of colors in the world."

"I know," Tiff replied. "We're really bummed."

"I'm with you one hundred percent on that!" I shot back. Linda gave me a look that said, "If you say one more word, you're gonna regret it later!" I shut up like a whipped pup.

An hour later, the call came again. This time, everyone listened closer to the Brit's pronunciation. Why everyone doesn't learn to speak American is beyond me. Once again, Linda and I bid the Essigs farewell, this time a bit more hastily.

Linda and I then settled in and relaxed. Later, we scanned the dock from our deck, attempting to spot our family and wave goodbye once again. A long line of folks descended the gangplank like snails, then entered a medical tent. Another long line crept out the tent onto the parking lot to load into buses headed for Travis AFB. Another long line of buses snaked out of the parking lot.

Unable to locate the Essigs, we went inside. Dinner arrived and we climbed into bed to view a movie we both wanted to watch—a much more difficult task than it may seem. I eventually convinced Linda to watch *For* v *Ferrari*, on the stipulation that we would both take in a chick flick the next day ... and I would pretend to like it, although the second condition would probably present an insurmountable challenge for me.

As I opened my mouth to chomp down on my burrito, that familiar knock resounded. Linda gave me a bewildered look and said, "It can't be." I opened the door, and sure enough it was. The whole Essig family stood before us, looking as if they had run a marathon.

Thankfully, once again I thought before speaking. Rather than expressing my disappointment at seeing them again, I managed to blurt, "What happened? Is everything okay?"

This time Scott spoke. "We got all the way to the end of the gangplank, and they shut down processing for the evening, just before we entered the medical tent."

I looked at the clock. They had waited in line with three small children for over two hours. I started to say, "We'll take Olive and Liam for you," but then remembered we always took them. Once again, I opened the hide-a-bed and tucked the two grandkids in for the night. They were too exhausted to even ask if they could watch a movie.

Later that night, Linda and I stepped outside on our deck. The sun was ablaze as it disappeared behind the skyline. To the west rose the impressive buildings of San Francisco, and to the east, those of Oakland. Breathtaking. Under normal circumstances, I would have said, "All is right with the world." But normal didn't exist anymore.

The next morning, everyone awoke much more refreshed. Except me. I stayed awake half the night wondering if Scott and Tiff's family would ever exit the boat. I was beginning to think we might have to attend the kids' high school graduations aboard the *Gran♦ Princess.*

Olive once again functioned as Queen Bee, issuing commands to all her subjects. Liam was in full-on Poop-Man mode, identifying everyone as "poo-poo head." Olin crawled across the hall with his parents into our room and immediately began destroying everything he could lay his hands on. That's why his parents dubbed him "Little Shredder." For a brief moment, I thought we were back home again.

"We were so exhausted last night," Tiff said, shaking her head.

"Pray tell, why?" I asked.

Tiff shot me a glance, under her breath muttering, "Don't start, Dad."

An hour or so later, their color and number were called once again. They got up and headed for the door. This time we all just waved at one another as the Essig family departed. Scott stopped in their room for one final inspection. Why? I wondered, certain they'd be back in a few minutes.

Only this time, they didn't return. They were off the ship, headed to Travis.

The captain announced that our color was at the front of the queue. But we waited and waited as color after color was called. I had agreed to the chick flick, only because I believed we would depart early. I regretted my decision. We finished one chick flick and were well into the second one. I don't recall the titles. Not that it matters; they all have the same plot. Then I received a phone call. Chip Franklin from KGO news radio wanted one more live interview before we left the ship.

I looked at Linda with feigned disappointment and expressed my regret that I would have to take a break from her movie. "As much as I hate to miss it, please don't stop the movie for me. I wouldn't want you to miss the good part. I might be a while."

"Okay." She smiled back at me, not at all fooled by my masquerade. I need to work on my acting skills, but after forty-six years of marriage, the extra practice probably wouldn't make any difference. Linda knows all my tricks.

A couple of minutes into Chip's interview, the call came. *The* call. The one we'd been anticipating ever since we docked at the Port of Oakland. Silver three could disembark. I celebrated the moment with Chip, explaining he had been fortunate enough to have me on the air live when I received the Queen Mother of phone calls. All his listeners could celebrate with us. He seemed totally underwhelmed.

Even though I had done so several times, I checked under the bed and in the closet to make sure we hadn't left anything. You never know. In the ten minutes since my last inspection, Linda may have kicked something under the bed. Scott and I share this obsession. Maybe that's why Tiff married him. To pick someone just like her daddy.

I turned on my phone. 5:00 p.m. Finally, we were leaving the ship. The bus ride would take forty-five minutes. The rest would be easy. We should be settled into our room at Travis by dark.

Chapter Twelve

FROM QUARANTINE TO QUARANTINE TO QUARANTINE

L   inda and I headed down the stairs because the elevator was packed tighter than a mosh pit at an Eagles' concert. We had expected to exit the ship fairly quickly. But arriving on deck five, we found the line to disembark extended beyond our view. I pulled out my handkerchief and wiped the sweat from my face. Looking around, I momentarily removed my mask so I could at least grab a couple of breaths. An hour and a half later, we arrived at the gangplank. But our victory was fleeting. We crept down the gangplank into the white medical tent. The staff inside were decked out in hazmat gear; clear plastic face coverings completed their fashionable ensemble. A CDC nurse took our temperatures, then allowed us to pass. I half-expected to receive some sort of rite-of-passage badge.

At this point, Linda and I were separated. A panel of medical officials from the WHO (World Health Organization) fired a series of questions at us with the rapidity of a tommy gun. Did we have a fever? Cough? Shortness of breath? Diarrhea? Were we covered head to toe in boils? Had we ever, over the course of our lives, been exposed to anyone who had any medical condition, no matter how trivial? Okay, it wasn't quite that comprehensive, but I felt as if I had the bubonic plague. The intimidation level was so high, I would have answered no to their questions even if I had walked into the tent, holding my head in my hands.

From there, the HHS (US Department of Health and Human Services) took over. Each official held a clipboard. (I'm confident it was merely a prop.) Their function was to probe into our personal life with every sort of question imaginable. What was my birthdate? Social security number? Address? Had I ever eaten green eggs and ham?

Besides the CDC, WHO, and HHS, the USAF (US Air Force), and the federal marshals, various officials from multiple institutions of the state of California were present. Most of them stood around looking as if their mother had just died from flesh-eating bacteria. Every now and then one of them flashed a badge at some poor unsuspecting soul, giving me the impression that any of us at any moment could be separated from the herd and cast into a bottomless pit.

My confidence in government bureaucracy plummeted to an all-time low. I nearly choked, knowing my tax dollars were being used so ineffectively. With all these government agencies working hand in hand, a person might assume *efficiency* was the watchword of the day. Not so. Each official wanted to be in charge, and not one of them yielded even a tiny bit of control for the sake of the unfortunate passengers potentially infected with this contagious malady.

Eventually, we were released to board a bus. A CDC official pointed to a bus, but just as the first person in our group began to climb the stairs, someone from the HHS waved us off and directed us to a different bus. Then a federal marshal stepped in and rerouted us to a third bus. The truth became as clear as an Alpine lake: the more government agencies involved in a project, the more incompetency rises—at an exponential pace.

Linda and I took our seats on the bus and waited for something to happen. Anything. But unless sitting on a bus is "something happening," nothing did. Some random man came on board, tore a piece of bright yellow tape off a roll, and placed it on each person's shoulder. I don't know what organization he worked for. As far as I knew, he could have been representing the

Justin Bieber fan club. The man also asked if everyone on board was a California resident. Two ladies in front told him they were from Georgia. He refused to give them a piece of yellow tape and told them they were on the wrong bus. Then I asked him the question I assumed was foremost in everyone's mind: "Why do we need a piece of yellow tape?"

"So the 'right people' will know you're from California," he said. Of course! Why did I even ask such a silly question? I was too frightened to ask who the "right people" were.

Then a woman from some unidentified government agency boarded our bus and told the ladies from Georgia they needed to be on a different bus. They started to cry. I looked at my fellow passengers and concluded that, by this point, pretty much all the rest of us were on the verge of tears as well. The woman told the Georgia ladies she'd be right back. Twenty minutes later, she returned and told them they could stay on the bus, but their luggage was on the way to Georgia. They'd have to wear dirty undies for the next two weeks.

After an hour and a half, our bus finally moved forward. As we approached the gate to leave the wharf, our driver pulled over. We sat for another hour as bus after bus passed us. Finally, the driver pulled out, made a U-turn, and circled back to our starting point. The woman who had made Georgia ladies cry boarded our bus once again and told them they had to get off and ride a different bus. We all groaned, and she shouted to us, "Okay. I'm sorry. I guess I'm a terrible person. Alright?"

I sensed that everyone on the bus was about to shout a hearty "amen!" But one person spoke up and said, "No, you're not a terrible person. Anyone could make a mistake." My dear wife. That's why I love her. She perpetually sees the good side of everyone and every situation (except with me, of course.) However, at this juncture of our journey, I don't believe anyone on the bus appreciated her optimism. The stress level was as high as Mt. Everest and spiraling upward with each passing second.

After the Georgia ladies and the government official had disembarked, the driver steered our bus out the gate onto the highway. Forty-five minutes later, we arrived at Travis Air Force Base. A sense of triumph permeated the bus. We had progressed from quarantine (on the ship) to quarantine (on the bus) to quarantine (at Travis AFB). As Linda and I left the bus, I thought, Thank God, there's no quarantine at home!

Chapter Thirteen

A SAUNA ON WHEELS

Our bus screeched to a halt at the curb behind two other buses. An Air Force sergeant came aboard, identified himself as our official host, and welcomed us. He possessed excellent people skills, speaking with kindness as he explained the intake process. When he finished, he turned to leave, then pivoted and said, "I know you've been through a lot. We'll do our best to get you off quickly. But you're probably going to be on the bus another hour and a half." Then he left.

That wasn't the news I wanted to hear or, judging from their facial expressions, the news any of my fellow passengers expected. However, one guy on board must have been happy because he gave the sergeant half a peace sign. Or maybe it was his special way of saying, "You're number one!" His wife loudly expressed her opinion that the sergeant was a "funny fellow"—or something with a lot of *F*s. Some folks just have to blame someone for situations they can't control.

It turned out the sergeant wasn't so good at telling time. His hour and a half turned out to be three and a half hours. There's no way to overstate the frustration or discomfort every person on the bus must have felt. Bus quarantine was brutal. All of us fanned ourselves frantically as our sweat collected on the floor in a communal pool. Fortunately, Linda fell asleep shortly after we arrived. But my restless leg syndrome kicked in and kept me awake.

At one point, I got up to use the restroom at the rear of the bus. "You probably don't want to go in there," a guy informed me.

"Why's that?"

"You'll find out." He was right. The light didn't work, but that was inconsequential because the door wouldn't close anyway. The smell and condition of the toilet seat would have failed third-world standards. Ironically, we had been quarantined on this bus out of concern over a communicable illness we may have contracted. But if using that toilet didn't curse me with a deadly plague, then my immune system possessed superpowers.

At last, the sergeant returned with good news. We could leave the bus. We jumped up to get off, but we needn't have hurried. Another slow line. Stepping off the bus, we were once again quizzed with the same questions we had been asked before boarding the bus. Then we were identified on the government list. There were a couple of more stations in the intake process I don't remember.

I glanced at my watch. 12:48 a.m. We were drunk with fatigue, but so were those serving us. They were doing their best, but for some of our fellow passengers, that wasn't good enough. I'm confident the one-fingered salute on our bus wasn't the only expression of frustration that evening.

But God loves to bless us, even in our most discouraging moments. The final stage of processing was room assignment. Linda and I approached the table and gave the lady our names. "I'm sorry, she said. "We have no rooms left in the hotel except one small room with two single beds. But we can put you in the apartments—"

"We'll take the apartment!" Linda said. The room-assignment lady handed her two key cards. Linda whisked me away before I could say another word. What a blessing! If we had not spent so many hours sweating in the sauna on wheels, we would have ended up in a hotel room rather than an apartment.

As we were leaving, another official said, "You can get your luggage over there." I looked in the direction he was pointing to and spied a mountain of suitcases and handbags.

We were asleep on our feet, so I asked, "Can we come back and get 'em tomorrow?"

He grunted out, "Yeah, right. There's gonna be even more luggage here tomorrow."

"Okay, Hon," I said to Linda, "Let's go look."

"I'll let you get it. I'm gonna lay down on that bench over there."

"But I can't …" Too late. She was already gone. I eventually located our six pieces of luggage and pulled them from the pile. I gave Linda her bags, then we dragged them over to the pickup point, where another bus would take us to our apartment.

"Linda, let's walk," I suggested. "It's only a half mile. We'll beat the bus." I was paranoid we might have to spend another six hours on the bus and feared we might lose our suitcases again after I had just rescued them from the Mt. Everest of luggage.

She gave me a look that said, "I wouldn't walk over there even if my only other choice was being dragged behind a camel." I begrudgingly boarded the bus, trusting we could locate our baggage when we disembarked.

From that point on, things were smoother than warm butter. The bus stopped at our apartment, and we retrieved our luggage, then dragged it up the stairs. Praise God, the key card worked. I've had a few run-ins with those beasts in the past. Our apartment was small but had everything we needed: a bed and a clean toilet.

I glanced at the clock as we collapsed on the bed. 1:57 a.m. We had left our room on the *Gran♦ Princess* at 5:00 p.m. A nine-hour procedure for a forty-five-minute bus ride! I'm convinced Princess Cruise Lines could have processed us in two hours flat if the government hadn't helped so much.

We were on dry land and in our new home. At least for the next two weeks.

Chapter Fourteen

LIFE ON THE BASE

L inda rolled over. "Could you bring me coffee?" she mumbled.

"Honey, we don't have any here, remember?"

She jerked upright and exclaimed, "Oh no!" as if she just learned her mother had died. "What are we going to do?"

"We'll find some ... somehow ... somewhere." But even as I spoke, I recognized the absolute futility of our situation. We had looked through the cabinets quickly the previous night. Now we pored through them like a miner panning for gold. Nothing. No coffee, creamer, cups, plates, or silverware. But one item we found in abundance ... toilet paper. Hilarious! While the rest of the world was fighting over TP, we were up to our rear ends in it.

We threw on some clothes and wandered the grounds around the apartments (wearing masks, of course). One question was on our lips: "Where can we find coffee?" Finally, a fellow traveler on the caffeine pilgrimage pointed us toward the laundry room. Each set of apartments had a laundry room which contained stackable bins. We rummaged through them like a dog digging up a bone.

We uncovered shampoo samples, packets of coffee creamer, and Styrofoam cups ... but no coffee. Trudging up our stairs in a state of futility, we encountered our neighbors. We mumbled the oft-repeated question, "Do you know where we can get coffee?"

"We found some coffee packets this morning. But we don't have any cups."

A smile spread across my face. "Well, we have cups but no coffee. Could we trade a little?" They burst forth with such joy, I felt like I'd offered them the Hope Diamond. Linda and I exchanged treasures with them and headed up to enjoy our morning cup of Joe.

Isn't it amazing how often we fail to appreciate the little things in life? When was the last time you got excited over Styrofoam cups or coffee packets? I'm guessing ... never! The time-worn cliché "you don't know what you've got till it's gone" rings true.

While we were ransacking the laundry room, my friend Arron called from Santa Rosa. A retired Navy commander, he and his wife, Charlene, were heading down to the PX at Travis. He wondered if they could bring us anything. His offer was like throwing a starving man a T-bone steak. Linda and I hurriedly put together a list, then called Kylie at our house so she could get the items ready for pickup. Arron and Charlene gathered the supplies from our house and arrived a couple of hours later. He called us from the front gate, where they had deposited several bags containing dishes, snacks, and ... instant coffee. Linda and I were a little closer to heaven. We also breathed a sigh of relief when we learned an hour later that the rules had changed and no one was allowed to receive items at the front gate.

After resolving the coffee issue, we called Tiffany. They were in the family unit – a 1400 square foot apartment located approximately 300 yards from our facility. The kids got on the phone and squealed with delight that none of them needed to share a bedroom. In addition, a full-scale playground stood outside their window. I couldn't help wondering how many bodily injuries would result from two overly-energetic children on the jungle gym.

My earlier preconceptions about the camp crumbled quickly. No barred windows, dim lights, or Spartan furniture. Our apartment was small, about 600 square feet, with a shower, kitchen-ette, and king-size bed. Two flat-screen TVs adorned the living room and bedroom walls. We weren't confined to quarters. We could walk the grounds of our complex whenever we wished, provided we wore our masks and stayed within the fence.

On our first day, we made a divine discovery—our balcony. Linda rejoiced that this enabled her to lie in the sun and tan portions of her body the solar rays never graced. Her delight evaporated when she realized the neighbors merely needed to peek around the corner to speak with us and all would be exposed.

The hot water in our room was another delight for Linda. She loved turning on the tap marked H and experiencing H_2O significantly warmer than the hot water emanating from pretty much every other faucet on the planet. Truthfully, the water was probably hot enough to scald the feathers off a chicken.

During our quarantine, the press interviewed one of our fellow residents. Her take on the experience was "We were forced against our will to be quarantined at a government facility surrounded by a fence, and if we tried to climb the fence, we would be arrested."

I suppose anyone could put some bizarre, negative spin on our situation and arrive at such a twisted version of truth. But Linda and I, along with the other quarantine mates we encountered, shook our heads in disbelief over such vomitus.

We walked around the grounds two or three times each day, not primarily for exercise but to get out of our apartment. Weaving our way along the sidewalks of the four apartment buildings in our complex, we averaged close to five miles each day. The poplars and post oaks provided shade on sunny days as we maneuvered across the freshly mown lawn.

On each outing, we encountered numerous residents. Of course, we all wore masks, making it difficult to indisputably identify each person we spoke with. But we all faced that challenge with grace. Quite a sense of camaraderie developed within our little community—the intimacy of a shared adventure. In virtually every conversation, someone mentioned how "crazy" the entire situation was. But the prevalent opinion among our community was that the press greatly exaggerated the difficulty of our experience.

Staying on a military base, we also enjoyed the patriotic experience of hearing reveille, Taps, and *The Star Spangle* *Banner* each day. Waking up to reveille our first morning was an almost ethereal experience. Taps was a peaceful reminder that "Day is done, gone the sun ..." We timed our evening stroll so we would be outdoors as the national anthem boomed across the base each evening at 5:00 p.m. People paused, removed head coverings (but not masks), and placed hands over their hearts. Such great symbolic gestures of the nation we love.

On Sundays we connected with our church back home (Santa Rosa Christian) via the internet. Our first Sunday at Travis, our church, along with thousands of others, began live streaming worship services. Each week we plugged in, and, in a small way, felt we were sitting in "our" pew, joining with our spiritual family in worship and the Word.

Linda and I enjoyed extra time each morning praying together. Rather than jumping out of bed and bolting out the door with our daily to-do list in hand, we eased into the day. For more than forty years, I've been able to predict Linda's first words after she awakens. She growls, "Barney, I need coffee." Since I live by the motto "Happy wife, happy life," I leap out of bed each morning and brew her a cup. Only I didn't have to brew her a cup at Travis because the tap water approached 212 degrees Fahrenheit, and we only had instant coffee. Nevertheless, after coffee duty, I headed to the living room and spent time in the Word, prayer, and meditation. Afterwards, Linda and I discussed what God had said to us. Those two hours felt like a taste of heaven.

A few days into our experience, a friend suggested that I send out regular video updates of our adventure. Regular turned into daily. Each morning I posted "My Encouraging Word" on Facebook. The tidbits took off like the jets we watched rising from the runways around us—some of them collected more than 2,000 views. I was humbled, knowing our experience encouraged so many others.

Somewhere in the middle of our quiet time each day, breakfast arrived. Pretty much always the same. Two boiled eggs, muffin, apple or banana, and two link sausages. The catering company the government employed could have exerted a tad more creativity. Lunch was either a salad with turkey or a turkey sandwich. Dinner selections were a bit more diverse, but I guess the main entrée in a third of our evening meals consisted of . . . turkey. Maybe someone in the Air Force base's food chain owned stock in a turkey farm.

After a few days, I got creative with our meals. We had a stockpile of boiled eggs, so I hoarded our mayo, mustard, and ranch dressing packets and created the ultimate dining experience—egg salad. A culinary delight.

Twice each day, medical officials took our temperature.

They zapped our foreheads with laser beams, then reported the results. On a couple of occasions, Linda's temperature registered on the high side. Completely understandable. I already was aware she was a bit of a hothead. Both times, we retrieved our digital under-the-tongue thermometer, which registered normal.

The base's chief medical officer was required to ask each of us if we desired to be tested for COVID-19. Her speech didn't exactly reach a Tony Robbins motivational level. She explained that the tests weren't 100 percent accurate, that anyone who tested positive would be sent to another part of the country and quarantined for two more weeks, and that there was a shortage of tests, hinting that anyone who wasn't experiencing symptoms should perhaps consider saying no. Linda and I joined the ranks of those declining to be tested.

Every afternoon at 2:00 p.m., all of us in quarantine were treated to the Town Hall Conference Call. I would have named it A Journey into Pooled Ignorance. The intent was to keep us updated on what was happening and to answer questions. I didn't need the call to tell me what was happening ... nothing! I suppose that's the reason folks lined up in the phone queue for two hours—to ask meaningless questions of the nice sergeant who first greeted us on the bus when we arrived. All I can say is he must have a martyr complex.

The two-week camp experience sort of melded into one memory as we routinely performed the same tasks each twenty-four-hour period. Our morning quiet time, then breakfast, followed by my "Encouraging Word" broadcast. Then our morning walk. Return to the room to read or text friends. Eat lunch. Go for another walk. Join the town hall conference call. Text friends.

Read some more. Eat dinner. Go for an evening walk. Shower. Text friends. Watch a movie. Text friends. Fall asleep. If the word *rut* comes to mind, I'm not surprised.

Like Bill Murray in *Groundhog Day*, Linda and I felt we were living the same day repeatedly. We also sensed we were catching a glimpse of our future in the wonderful world of assisted living. Meals delivered to our room, undue medical attention, and walks around the grounds. But we knew we would return home soon and once again move about as freely as we wished.

Chapter Fifteen

HOME AGAIN

March 23. Waiting. We'd had our fair share of it. But we were scheduled to go home the following day. That final-day-of the-trip-I-can't-wait-to-get-home anxiety pumped through my veins. At 3:00 p.m. I stood in the living room of our apartment listening to the town hall conference call while I checked my Facebook messages and attempted to stay awake. Then I heard it. "We have just received word that the CDC has lifted restrictions for all passengers who have arranged private transportation. They are allowing you to leave today at five p.m."

Wait a second, I thought. That's us. Did he just say we could leave today? I started to shout into the receiver, "Repeat that!"

Then the CDC officer said, "Let me repeat that." Sure enough, he repeated it. And sure enough, the officials were allowing us to go home a half day early. I looked around. Clothes were scattered everywhere. We had only started to think about packing. All our food was in the cabinets. The fridge was crammed with perishables. The garbage needed dumping. No way could we possibly be ready in a couple of hours. Linda was in the bedroom. I started to get her attention, then my cell phone buzzed.

"Dad, did you just hear? We can leave today. Scott and I just discussed it. He wants to get home right away."

My mind flashed to the memory of the last time we saw the kids. Linda came up with the brilliant idea that we should simultaneously come out of our apartments, find the closest point, and see if we could spot one another. So we did. Sure enough there stood their family. As we looked across a field spanning three hundred yards, we saw them, waving and jumping, as we spoke on the phone. Even from that distance, I could see Olive and Liam practicing their Kung Fu moves on each other's heads. No wonder Scott wanted to leave as soon as possible.

Linda entered the room. "They're letting us leave early if we want," I said. "Scott and Tiff are going. We only have a couple of hours. I don't think we can do it."

She snatched the phone from my hand faster than a five-legged tomcat running from a prairie brush fire. "Yes, we're going too." Forget about asking me. Forget about the fact that she hadn't heard any details from the town hall conference call. Forget about the fact that our room was a disaster. My princess had spoken. We were leaving the base in two hours.

One phone call to Kylie and Bennie confirmed their availability to pick us up. I was relieved. When Linda sets her mind to something, the Great Wall of China can't block her from achieving it.

Sure enough, we closed the door to our apartment at 4:55 p.m. Dragging our luggage down the sidewalk, we handed the official our key cards and walked outside the fence for the first time in two weeks. It was merely a four-foot chain link fence, but inhaling the air of freedom outside the Travis gate felt fresher. I could almost hear the *Rocky* theme song "Gonna Fly Now," playing softly in the background.

I was more than a bit concerned as we took our seats on the bus. Our last bus ride had resulted in a three-hour quarantine in jungle-like humidity. But this time we hit the road in fifteen minutes. Pulling out, I suggested to our fellow passengers that we ask our driver to stop so we could all buy turkey sandwiches. They serenaded me with a chorus of jovial boos.

The first thing I noticed in the real world was the price of gas, which had dropped by nearly a dollar—a tidbit of news we had missed because the media was obsessed with the coronavirus.

Kylie and Bennie picked us up at the drop-off point, and on our way home, I noticed something else that had changed during our confinement—the traffic. Or the lack thereof. At 6:00 p.m. on a weeknight, Interstate 80 should have been packed with vehicles. Instead, it was as devoid of traffic as the surface of Mars.

We stopped and grabbed burgers to go because takeout was our only dining choice. Another huge change—no inside dining. I noticed lines of red tape on the floor. "What's the tape for?" I naively asked the clerk.

"Whoa, dude. Are you for real? It's for social distancing," he replied through his mask. I started to ask the meaning of "social distancing" but decided I didn't need additional reprimands from a dude who was missing half his teeth. More insane changes in my comfortable little world.

Then as we pulled away, I fought a moment of panic. "Kylie, do we have any toilet paper at home?"

"Yes ... and it's a good thing. You can't find it anywhere in the stores."

The world had gone nutty while we were gone. I made a mental note: Never leave home again.

We made it to our house in record time. Our Boston terrier, Chloe, nearly knocked us over when we opened the front door. I stepped into the backyard. Our lawn looked like a jungle from a *Jurassic Park* set. We had not expected Bennie to mow the lawn, but I didn't realize grass could grow that much in five weeks. It felt weird being home—no need to wear a mask every time we exited our abode, no meal delivery. But it felt good. We were home.

After Linda checked on her animals and watered her plants, she retreated to the bathroom and turned on the tap to the Jacuzzi bathtub. After two weeks of showering, she was ready for a warm soak.

We had gone from quarantine (on the ship) to quarantine (on the bus) to quarantine (on the base) to quarantine (in the world).

Epilogue

Two days after Linda and I returned home, Michael and Dana Bryant from Crossing the Jordan (CTJ) laid me off from my position, along with most of the other paid employees. The industries that provide their income (primarily thrift stores) were considered nonessential by the local government and were forced to close. Abortion clinics and marijuana dispensaries are considered essential, but a Christian ministry providing housing and a new life to 120 adults and children—consisting of former prostitutes, criminals and addicts—is nonessential. The city might whistle a different tune if the people who are housed at CTJ take to the streets and resume their criminal activity.

Michael and Dana are incredibly resourceful and thus far continue operating the program. I remain in contact with the staff and "kids"—a term Linda and I lovingly use to describe the program members. Within six weeks of returning home, I performed two weddings for CTJ graduates—in a backyard and on a beach. More weddings are coming. The beauty of life continues, despite quarantine.

Our store, The Bird's Nest, has been closed since March 15. After twenty-eight years in business, we face the realistic possibility of permanent shutdown. At that point, we may have no choice but to leave California for financial reasons. It would be heartbreaking to say goodbye to our grandchildren and our farm.

However, for the present, God continues to provide financially in amazing ways. He's shown us ways to trim our budget. Our savings, unemployment checks, and the online store sales keep us afloat.

Interviews with the media trickled in for a few weeks after we returned. But now we're old news. The media has moved on to hotter stories.

Scott's job as an electronic security technician was deemed essential. Tiffany joined the wonderful world of home schooling. Linda acquired two new goats and now spends hours sitting with them in our field. I continue to broadcast "Today's Encouraging Word" three times weekly.

In many ways, The Corona Cruise adventure seems like a distant dream. Linda and I are still the same people, yet we have changed in several ways. The lessons we learned from those five weeks will stay with us the rest of our lives.

Friends ask, "How did you survive quarantine?" Truthfully, we not only survived it but, in many ways, thrived in isolation.

First, we learned to trust God in new ways. Scriptures heralding messages such "wait on the Lord,"[1] "trust in the Lord with all your heart,"[2] and "all things work together for good,"[3] are more than refrigerator-magnet verses for us now. They're living re-

---

[1] Isaiah 40:31 NKJV

[2] Proverbs 3:5 NIV

[3] Romans 8:28 NKJV

alities, permanently engraved on our hearts. One of our biggest challenges was facing continual uncertainty. But uncertainty is where God wants us to live, because that's the place where we learn to trust Him.

Second, we discovered what it means to live in the moment. The book of Lamentations states, "His mercies... are new every morning."[4] Jesus commands us, "Do not worry about tomorrow. For tomorrow will care for itself."[5] And he prayed, "Give us this day our daily bread."[6] Thriving throughout our five-week adventure required us to remain in the moment, living one day at a time, because that's the only reality that exists.

Third, we realize we must accept what is. The Serenity Prayer states, "God, grant me the serenity to accept the things I cannot change, the courage to change the things I can, and the wisdom to know the difference." Reality is reality. It is what it is. Complaining about things we can't change creates a living hell. But when we accept reality and view each moment of our lives as a beautiful gift from God, we step into heaven on earth.

Finally, practicing gratitude for life's simple blessings is one of the greatest joys we can experience. If we focus on what we don't have, we miss out on what we do have. The writer of Ecclesiastes repeatedly challenges us to enjoy whatever simple blessings God gives us: food, shelter, family, and faith. Wallowing in entitlement and self-pity kills our joy faster than a speeding bullet.

Linda and I continue to be amazed at the ways God worked

[4] Lamentations 3:22–23 HCSB

[5] Matthew 6:34 NASB

[6] Matthew 6:11 NASB

through us on our trip. Almost from the beginning, we sensed God had a purpose for us on this voyage. God in His sovereignty chose us to be on the Grand Princess.

No one in the family will forget our thirty-two-day adventure (well, except for Olin, who remained clueless through the entire ordeal). And we all thank God for what we have today. We don't know what lies over the next hill on our journey through life. But we know God will be there, waiting for us, just as he was during The Corona Cruise.